THE FACE I MADE

When The Doctor Said I Had Cancer... Again!!!

by

Jonathan & Regina Newby

Jai Publishing House Incorporated
1230 Peachtree Street NE, 19th Floor
Atlanta, Georgia 30309
www.jaipublishing.com

Printed in the United States of America

ISBN-13: 978-1-7366613-0-7

In loving Memory of

Jonathan Newby
Forever My Sweet Daddy

Dedication

There are so many people to whom I want to dedicate this book.

...

First, I would like to thank my wife, *Regina Newby*. Thank you for all your love and support. Thank you for driving me batshit crazy, fussing over me. Being my social worker, cook, personal nurse, and chauffeur. I love you to the moon and back, Honey.

Next, I want to thank my two sons, *Alex* and *Braxton*. You are two great sons and I thank God for you. I'm so excited for your future, and so proud of the young men you are growing into.

Thanks to my parents, *John* and *Dr. JoAnne Newby*, for all of your love and support through all of this cancer stuff.

I want to give a big shout out to *Keffery* and *Delisia Evans*. Ya'll been my ride or die peeps for real.

And thanks to all of my friends and family for all of the support—even the small things, like cooking or buying dinner, hospital and home visits, phone calls, texts, messages on Facebook, and love offerings.

Last but not least, I want to thank the team of Doctors and Nurses that saved my life twice! My Oncologist, Dr. Gillum Qureshi; and the Bone Marrow Transplant Team at MCV Massey Cancer Center.

| By Arielle S. Newby

Foreword

To the readers, I am beyond honored to write the foreword for this book. My uncle J.O. was (is) one the most important men in my life.

I never really knew my biological father and between J.O. and my grandfather, I never missed a beat. My uncle J.O. met Regina on a blind date.

I knew the two of them would be together forever from the moment I met Regina.

As a child, I was very attached to my uncle and instantly developed the same natural attachment to

Regina. At their wedding, of course, I was the junior bride. I was around nine or ten years old.

When they said "I do", I *naturally* expected I would go everywhere with them, especially their honeymoon. I quickly learned that was not happening and raised hell upon being told "no".

Everyone said I was being dramatic; I beg to differ. This was one of the most depressing moments of my life and I still have not forgiven them.

…

My uncle and aunt are amazing people. Their story is one of love, endurance and compassion. This story is easily the best testament to what marriage means and what it takes to make it.

We often think it's just the beauty of the wedding day, but it is so much more.

Foreword

I write this foreword hoping this book will inspire, motivate, and create an understanding that every moment, every minute counts – even the final second.

From the world's greatest and most loving niece,

Arielle S. Newby

Arielle S. Newby

Contents of Our Story

THE FACE I MADE

When The Doctor Said I
Had Cancer... Again!!!

by

Jonathan & Regina Newby

"

When I dare to be powerful – to use my strength in the service of my vision, then it becomes less and less important whether I am afraid. – Audre Lorde

"

Prologue

Let me first start by introducing myself.

> *Hi, I'm Jonathan Newby. I'm a Virgo, and I like long, romantic walks on the beach.*

> …

I bet you thought this was going to be one of those uplifting, feel-good, triumph-over-cancer stories.

In a way, it is… being that I'm still alive to write this book using my own words, narrating my own story.

◆

If there is one thing you should know about me… Warning: Disclaimer… I Own My Shit!

I have accepted my duality. There is a part of me that is a responsible, caring, empathetic adult. The other half, well yeah, I'm a Bro—that part of me that demands my action movies to have fast cars, big explosions, and women with even bigger tits! It has a totally inappropriate sense of humor and juvenile.

So yeah, I feed the beast; and so at any given time during the course of this book, I'm going to say some outlandish shit!

◆

Now you have noticed the title of this book… the key words being *Cancer* and *Again*. That's right, I loved Cancer so much I got it twice!

It is safe to say that the last three years of my life totally sucked. Don't get me wrong, I've learned a lot about myself and life in general, but I can think of easier ways to learn those lessons.

I thank God for my wife, kids, parents and friends. I have an awesome support system that helped me through this journey.

Sincerely,

Jonathan

| By Jonathan Newby

Part 1: My 40s Sucked

Chapter 1: Can't Lift Squat!!

It is late spring of 2012, and I am excited about turning 40. I had a side hustle baking and sold my cookies, Sweet Daddyz Cookiez.

I was starting to work out at the gym. I ran my first 10k earlier in the year, and was coaching youth league football. I even started participating in powerlifting competitions at the gym.

◆

When I put all of that on paper, I realized I had a pretty busy life. Wolfgang's Gym is loaded with award-winning bodybuilders and fitness models. I'm not one of those guys that get all intimidated when he sees a guy with bigger muscles and washboard abs.

I use that as motivation. I don't want to be at a gym where everyone looks like me. I love lifting, and when I'm in the gym, I have no worries.

I'm not a big goal setter; back in college, I made a New Year's resolution to stop making New Year's resolutions. Needless to say, I made that resolution over twenty years ago and still keeping it to this very day.

But I did make fitness goals, and as funny as it may seem, I started to make more life goals for myself after I came face-to-face with my own mortality.

…

But back to me being a gym rat… I set a goal to bench press 400 pounds. 'Join the 400 club' was my mantra.

It was in the gym and at work where I noticed that my energy levels were a little off. At work, I started to feel fatigued and lightheaded.

I work in a warehouse environment, chucking boxes to and fro all night. After a few weeks, something told me to check my temperature.

To my surprise, it was 101°. It was puzzling, but did not raise any red flags for me. I just popped some ibuprofen and toughed it out.

...

It didn't take long for me to notice that my workouts were getting tougher. I usually end my bench press sets with one rep of 315 pounds. On this particular day, I was doing my bench presses when one of the female trainers walked into the free weight section with three female clients. By that time, I was on my last set, which means I get to slap on 345-pound plates on the bar.

Now, I was not trying to show off in front of the women, but I was hoping that they noticed me pushing up the massive weights.

And low and behold, I made a complete ass of myself when the weight went down and sat there on my damn chest.

It took two guys to lift the weight off my chest. "What the fuck just happened?" I thought to myself, a little taken back. And, of course all the commotion drew the trainer and her clients' attention.

"You okay?" the trainer asked me. "Yeah," I replied. "You usually lift a lot of weight," she said with a slightly amused look on her face. "I know," I said, "and in front of your clients, too."

"Aww, don't worry about it. You're just having an off day," she said as she was walking away. I admit it; I took in a huge eye full of the trainer's ample posterior as she walked away. See, I always find a silver lining!

◆

Even though I just passed it off as an 'off day' like the trainer said, it still bothered me that I could not complete this simple routine.

I just chalked it up to getting old, I guess. Completely unaware of what fun stuff is brewing inside my body.

...

Later on that summer, it was time to get ready for the upcoming football season for the youth football league I coached.

One Saturday, I had a football clinic, a bench press and deadlift competition. So I did the clinic that morning, and left to go to the gym to participate in the lifting competition.

When I got to the gym, I was feeling fine—nothing to be concerned about. I felt confident because last year I maxed out at 350 pounds, so I was sure to have a decent performance today and beat my personal best.

My goal was 360 pounds. Unofficially I hit 365, but I bounced the weight off my chest, which was not allowed in the competition.

I did my first lift of 300 pounds. It was a successful lift, but it took a little out of me. That weight usually did not feel that heavy to me. I always do one rep of 315, after doing three full sets when I did bench presses.

A feeling of concern came over me. That first lift was supposed to be a confidence booster. When it came time for my second lift, I thought, "Okay, it's time to throw up some big boy weight. I only have three attempts, and I want to break my personal record."

...

I decided to at least tie my personal best from last year's competition, and moved up to the 350-pound lift.

As soon as my spotter gave me the lift-off, I knew something was wrong. I brought the weight down. I was confident in my position on the bench and handgrip on the bar, and my overall technique; but it did not feel like the weight that I remembered.

When the judge gave the command to lift, I could not get the weight more than a few inches off my chest.

That second burst of strength and movement when you start engaging more muscle groups did not come. When it was obvious that I would not get this weight up, I nodded for my spotter to help me rack the weight.

Needless to say, it was a confidence buster! When it came time for my third lift, it was déjà vu all over again. I was humiliated.

A guy my size of 270 pounds only lifting 350, I wanted to just sit in a corner and hang my head in shame.

◆

Even when it came time for the deadlift portion of the competition, I just played it safe and ended my third lift at 425 pounds.

The guys from the gym were saying, "If you were outside all morning in the sun, that would zap your energy. It would help if you had plenty of rest before a competition."

I just told myself that I was doing too much. I should've just done one event instead of both events at the same time.

Lesson learned…

“

*It always seems impossible until
it's done.* – Nelson Mandela

”

Chapter 2: I Am An Alcoholic and I Have Mono!!

It's getting near to the end of summer, and football practice is just getting started. I've started to notice that I start to feel a little weak and feverish late in the afternoon, but I just chalked it up to the scorching heat, my busy schedule, and my age.

...

I was just about to turn 40, you know! Even at work toward the end of my shift, I felt drained. I really did not think anything of it, and just kept on trucking.

By mid-August, my wife and I started this weight loss program, and I wanted to look lean and sexy for my

40th birthday in September. You know, just drop about five pounds a month, nothing major.

I also knew that I needed to get my annual health physical—plus I was turning 40, that meant I had to get the dreaded finger!!!! I was not looking forward to that. I'm talking about a prostate exam.

If you are a 40-year-old male, or know one that has not had a prostate exam, please encourage them to get one.

...

So a couple of weeks go by, and I started to slim down a little. Nothing drastic, plus I was trying to shed a few pounds anyway, so no alarm bells.

I do my weigh-ins with my wife, and everyone in the program was all happy about my progress.

So September 8th hits… that is my birthday, y'all, and I'm just going along like everything's A-Okay.

A week later, I had my annual physical exam, and I didn't think anything of it. Just a regular routine check-up, or so I thought.

A few days later, the doctor's office called me to come back to do some follow-up testing. The nurse on the phone told me that my liver functions were 'off'.

◆

A couple of days later, I went back to the doctor's office so he could run more tests. When I came for my follow-up test, it was with another doctor. He wanted to test me for Mononucleosis.

My reaction was, "Mono?? Like in the kissing disease?? What I look like, some horny high school teen? How in the world would I get Mono?"

The doctor had one working theory. My primary care doctor had another theory. I was getting tested for everything under the sun, because I showed multiple symptoms.

After the passing of another week, I went back to the doctor's office. In the office, the doctor asked more questions about my lifestyle habits, mainly alcohol consumption.

My answer to this question as long as I can remember has always been *three to four beers a week*. But this time, I felt that he did not believe me... he gave me *that look*.

Apparently, I showed symptoms of Cirrhosis of the liver—a liver disease caused by—yep, you guessed it —excessive alcohol consumption.

...

Now at this point, I was starting to feel feverish at work. I rarely ran a fever and didn't quite know what it was that I was feeling. All I know is that I was starting to feel weak and hot towards the end of my work shift.

This went on for another three or four weeks before I just decided, *Hey, maybe I should check my temperature. Usually, around 6 o'clock in the evening, I will start to feel a little warm and feverish, so I will check my temperature then.*

I started to notice that my temperature would be over 100°. When I told my doctors that I was starting to run fevers, they still had many theories of different diseases that I may have. Still mono was the one disease that topped the list of possible illnesses.

…

Weeks turned into months, and now my temperature was starting to spike up to 102°. At this point, I was starting to call out sick because I was feeling too weak to go to work.

My doctor then referred me to an oncologist—they figured that I must have a blood disease.

When I started going to my oncologist, they started running a whole battery of tests to rule out any other disease. I was tested for everything, including AIDS, which really shocked the hell out of me.

I thought back to every female I had any kind of physical intimate contact with, from the time I was a kid in elementary school to a full-grown adult.

While I was being pricked and probed, I was still able to work whenever I felt well enough. I worked through the busiest season of the year, which was Thanksgiving and Christmas.

There were times when I had to call out because my fever was high; and other times I felt well enough to work a full shift. Pretty much, I felt like Pac-Man—the way I was swallowing ibuprofen.

...

I would go to the emergency room so often now that the nurses in the emergency room started to recognize me, and I started to recognize them.

I felt some kind of way when I see the "Big Bang Theory" television show, because it was around that time in the evening when my fever wood spike high and I would end up in the emergency room. Like clockwork.

◆

I'd noticed that I was losing weight, but that didn't alarm me because I was trying to lose weight anyway. But my energy level was starting to fall, and I noticed that particularly when I was still coaching youth football.

Unfortunately, the last two games of the season, I just did not feel well enough to go to any of the games.

But around November, I did feel well enough to make one of the playoff games when the coaches noticed I was losing weight. But again, I will still trying to lose weight, and it did not quite register that my weight loss was due to something else.

◆

So I worked through Thanksgiving, Christmas and New Year's, still going back and forth to doctor's appointments - and the emergency room - and work.

Around February, I was at the gym with my youngest son. Braxton took a picture of me on one of the weightlifting equipment.

When I saw the picture, I was alarmed to see how round my stomach looked... as if I had a ball under my shirt.

I found this kind of odd, but thought, "Okay, I'm just losing weight, but it's still kind of slow going around my midsection."

Later on that week, I was at work, and I started having severe abdominal cramping; it was almost to the point where I could barely stand up straight.

I struggled to finish my shift, and when I left, that would be the last time I would walk back into the building for another 6+ months.

"

Don't watch the clock; do what it does. Keep going.
– Sam Levenson

"

Chapter 3: I'm Full Of It!!

Later on that evening, once again, I found myself in the emergency room. This time I complained of abdominal pain, so the doctors ordered more x-rays.

That was when the doctors found fluid in my abdomen. The emergency room doctor considered admitting me into the hospital, but wanted to first consult with my oncologist, Dr. Qureshi.

My oncologist did not want to admit me to the hospital because the infection risk was too high with my weakened immune system. Of course, with my luck, that all happened on a Friday night, which meant I had to wait until Monday to get the fluid pumped out of my stomach.

...

Monday came, and I went to Dr. Qureshi's office to have my abdominal area examined. At that point, he scheduled a procedure called *paracentesis* to extract a sample of body fluid from my abdomen. This procedure would completely change my life as I knew it!

I made my way into this small examination room, and the doctor there took an ultrasound of my abdomen. There he could see the pouch of fluid in my abdomen, and that is exactly where he performed the *paracentesis* procedure to remove the fluid from my abdomen.

This was undoubtedly one of the most painful procedures I've ever experienced in my life, and it was something that I had to go through 4 more times before I was finally diagnosed with cancer.

...

The nurse I had for those *paracentesis* procedures was awesome; she did all she could to make my experience as bearable and comfortable as possible.

One of the first things the doctor did was to numb the area in which he would insert this tube to drain the fluid. The epidural felt like tiny bee stings in my abdomen.

Next, the doctor told me that I would feel some *pressure* and hear a popping sound. Let me tell you that *pressure* was NOT the word I would've used to describe once I heard that pop.

There was a big, rapid sensation in my abdomen that was just something I'd never experienced before in my life.

The whole procedure took all of 15 minutes, but it was the longest 15 minutes of my life. The fluid that came out of me looked just like beer, which was befitting since I felt like a keg that had just been tapped.

...

After draining about a half-gallon of fluid from your abdomen, you'll be surprised how hungry you get!

Now the first time I went through this process, it was something that I could tolerate. It was okay, but it didn't take long for this process to get real old, real quick.

After being drained through paracentesis five times... that fifth time, you're done.

"

If you change the way you look at things, the things you look at change. – Wayne Dyer

"

Intercession

To watch our love story movie style and on the big screen, access the video here:

Oh, and you will need this password: lovestory

bit.ly/newbyfamily2020

| By Regina Newby

Part II: Life After Jonathan

Chapter 4: Weird Labs

My husband had a health physical in September. The results came back the following week, and the doctor said that he wanted J.O. to come back for more labs—his liver counts were high. The appointment was set to go back and run more tests.

In between that visit, my husband and I were at a café having a smoothie, and he started to feel really dizzy. He told me what was happening and that he didn't think he could drive.

He also said he was hot, so I started fanning him to try to cool him off; but it wasn't working. He didn't look good and I was concerned.

I called 911, and he was sent to the hospital. Little did we know, that was the beginning of a 7-year nightmare.

◆

While J.O. was in the emergency room, his bloodwork was done, and vitals were taken. He had a temperature, and his blood work again stated his liver counts were high. He was released and advised to follow up with his primary care.

…

For several months, culture samples and various lab tests were done; and still, no one had any answers.

What was causing his fevers all day? He could only take ibuprofen to bring the fever down.

After a few months, his primary care physician referred him to a hematologist. It was not until then that after more labs and bone marrow tests were done, we learned that J.O. had Large B Cell lymphoma.

At that moment, in some ways, I felt relieved.

I mean, *cancer* was not what any of us wanted to hear, but at least we now had a name to what had him feeling sick for over the past year. My relief came from *knowing,* now we can fix it. We can find out what to do to make him well again.

In a way, I know my husband was relieved because whatever treatment was next, it had to be better than getting procedures done every 7 days for draining fluid from his body.

Yes, a few weeks before the cancer diagnosis, my husband's stomach began retaining fluid, and I mean a *lot* of fluid to the point he was having back pain.

Every week he had to go to the hospital and have a catheter shoved into his stomach, and drained sometimes 10-12 pounds of fluid from his abdomen.

That is the procedure he talked about as being the worst pain he had ever experienced (in his chapter earlier).

I was in the room for one of the procedures, and I literally wanted to cry when I saw that he almost jumped off the table when the catheter was pushed in his abdomen. I never saw my husband in pain like that.

Can you imagine a catheter that has barbed grooves on each side pushing through your stomach to drain fluid?

At that moment, I physically felt sick to my stomach because it hurt me so bad to see him going through that pain. I kept my composure to stay strong for him.

…

After 6 months of back-and-forth to doctor visits, blood works, and culture samples, we had a diagnosis and a treatment plan. My husband started chemo treatments, and even after the first treatment, he began to feel better over the next couple of weeks.

When he went for his first chemo treatment, we had no idea of the process as far as time. You see, chemo treatments can literally be all day sometimes. I had to drop him off at the hospital, drop my kids off at school, and then I could go back to be with him at chemo.

His first bag would take about an hour, then the second bag about another two hours or so, only to be followed by two more bags of chemo about 30 minutes each.

Yes, you read correctly, so now you have entered the world of chemo.

...

My long days consisted of being at a treatment center, lots of back-and-forth driving, and tiredness. After six chemo sessions, he was done. They did follow-up scans and bloodwork. He was in remission.

Praise God! We were both so happy. To think how grim things were and then to finally have this disease gone was a blessing.

And then...

"

You were made by God and for God, and until you understand that, life will never make sense.
– Rick Warren

"

Chapter 5: A New Normal, We Thought

After all that we had been through, we tried to get some type of normalcy to our lives. To be honest, there really is never a normal life after cancer.

For about 2 years, my husband was doing great. He felt good, and I saw him laugh and enjoy life again. Well, as you can guess, things one day changed.

Some of the ugly symptoms began to show their ugly face. He started having fevers and coughing again. His urine color also changed. After two years of feeling free from cancer, it was confirmed that the lymphoma was back. This time a bone marrow transplant was recommended.

…

In 2016, J.O. had an autologous bone marrow transplant. I think the worst part for him was getting mucositis because of the strong chemo.

Mucositis causes dark sores on the inside and sometimes outside of the mouth. They are very painful.

For about 3 days after the transplant, my husband could not talk because it hurt so bad. He said that even eating a popsicle hurt, so you can imagine the suffering he went through in the days of recovery.

◆

He stayed in the hospital for about 3 weeks; and then he was released but still had to go to the clinic every day.

J.O. was closely monitored so suddenly our lives became a series of doctors appointments and tests, paying close attention to fluids, potassium, blood work, etc.

As the doctor patiently explained what to expect after the hospital stay, all that was running through my mind was how we would do all of this.

I started mentally planning how I would get my husband to his appointments and still try to go to work myself.

See, the first time my husband was diagnosed with cancer, he was out of work for 6 months. This time, it was 8 months.

So many thoughts were running through my head. Feelings of not being able to be by his side for every single appointment. I feared not being a good mom.

How was I going to handle all of this without my ride or die? All kinds of worries began to crowd my mind all in a matter of minutes as I sat there with J.O. trying to listen to the doctor—but still my mind was busy trying to make sense of it all.

...

You might ask why I would think about those things? Well, the reality was this: I knew I had to get my husband to these appointments, but because he wasn't physically able to work, I also knew there would be times I would have to work around clinic visits.

And not to mention the bills. I realized I had to put money in our household so we could eat and pay bills.

I did not know exactly *how* I would do it, but I knew I would be there for my husband no matter what. After that doctor's visit, I heard about a caregiver class. I decided I wanted to take the caregivers class to know everything I could know on how to take care of J.O. after his transplant.

…

During this class, we learned about the importance of being a caregiver and the role you play in making sure it is a smooth transition from the hospital to home. The hospital also taught nutrition and how to prepare your house before your loved one comes home.

I must say, I learned a lot during this class! I learned I had to remove all live plants from the inside of the home, and make sure the home is as clean as possible.

Basically, give a thorough spring cleaning. You see, for a patient who has recently had a transplant, the germ is a huge no-no—your loved one's immune system is already compromised.

I had to learn how to prepare food before serving it to J.O. For instance, if I bought deli meat for a sandwich, it had to be put in the microwave for a few seconds to help kill any germs that could be from someone handling it beforehand.

I thought to myself, *Wow*! Something that I've done a million times now has a whole new meaning.

Curious about the deli meat, I asked the trainer, "So this sounds like something *everyone* should do anyway, right?"

She without hesitation responded, "Yes, it would be a good idea."

To this very day, I practice the same method of ridding the deli meat from germs by zapping it in the microwave first.

…

Another thing I learned was that all of the meals had to be home-cooked, no fast food. Yes, that was a big one, especially for a busy family like we were. The convenience of fast food had met its end.

That caregiver class was a lot to take in, but highly informative. J.O. asked me about the class, and I jokingly said, "It was good. Chef Newby is ready."

Of course, he laughed and said, "Yeah right!"

He laughed because even though I can cook, my husband absolutely loved cooking. My thought was, hey, if he loves it, I will not get in his way. Lol!

You could say I was a spoiled wife. Waking up on Sunday mornings and your husband is in the kitchen cooking breakfast or making dinner for you, of course you would be spoiled.

I loved seeing him come up with new dishes for the family. My man at the stove cooking was all the way sexy for me.

....
I admit I miss his funny jokes. My husband was hilarious.
....

So after being home a few days, the Mother's Day weekend was approaching. That morning, we were sitting at the table eating breakfast, and we heard a knock at our door. My husband answered the door, and it was one of our neighbors.

She said, "You might want to come to look at your car, someone hit it."

Now I was thinking maybe a little ding, no big deal. Oh no, I was so wrong! We walked to my car on the passenger's side, and I said, "What the hell?!" The door was partially bent in so that it had popped out the top.

My car had been hit so hard, it actually shifted over in the driveway. Looking at the car, we both said, "Wow!" Then I said, "Is someone punking us?"

J.O. had just gotten out of the hospital, and now our car was hit in our own front yard. WTH! I remember saying, "Lord, can we just catch a break?"

…

I called the police and filed a report—to no avail. To this day, we never found out who hit our car.

That same day my insurance company towed the car to a dealership to have it looked at by an adjuster. A few days later, I talked to the adjuster, and he said, "Well, Mrs. Newby, unfortunately, we had to total your car."

He said we were already at $5,000 worth of damage, so it wasn't worth going any further at that point. He told us whoever hit our car, hit it with so much force on the impact that it destroyed the frame.

J.O. had said the same thing when he saw a dent at the very bottom of the door.

I told the adjuster that I could buy another car, but I was grateful that my car was always parked on that side of the driveway. It actually blocked the other driver from hitting the house where our two kids' bedrooms were. What seemed like a bad thing, actually worked out for our good. The Lord had our backs on this one, too.

It was such a great testimony that the adjuster was taken aback at what happened. He exclaimed, "I gotta tell my wife about this because I would call that Divine intervention!" I said, "You're exactly right."

...

Now we were down to one vehicle, but that was okay because the situation could have been so much worse. After that whole mess with the car being totaled, even though we had one vehicle, we worked it out. We were such a good team together. We faced challenges together, as long as we were together.

Thankfully a few months later, a good friend of ours sold us her mom's old car for pretty much pennies. We were thankful just to get another vehicle.

So as months passed, J.O. was doing well. I was happy because even though the bone marrow transplant was risky, he handled it well physically. To see him begin to look and feel like himself again was a blessing. If that was what it took to heal him from lymphoma, it was worth it.

...

In the summer of 2017, I was chosen to be on a hair design team to style hair for the models participating in a big fashion show in New York. Honestly, I was happy to be picked.

As I was trying to figure out travel plans, I really didn't want to fly to New York by myself and have to rent a car to get to the only hotel I even knew about—and it was an expensive hotel! I didn't know much else about New York.

So I talked to my husband about it and he said, "If you want, I can take a vacation day and go with you."

Excitedly I said, "That will be fun, so let's do it!" And planning commenced.

We went into strategizing our impromptu getaway. We made plans to rent a car and stay with my cousin in New Jersey, instead of paying for a hotel room stay in New York. That solved my problem with that expensive hotel, plus it saved us money.

New Jersey was close enough to get to my hair show, but far enough not to deal with the New York traffic. So far, so good.

It was finally time to head to New York, and for some reason, we couldn't get a rental car for the time we needed, so J.O. says, "We are taking the white car."

I said, "You think it will make it?"

He said, "We got a fresh oil change; let's fill the car and go."

All I kept thinking was if some idiot hadn't hit my car and totaled it, we could be driving my car, which was newer and more comfortable than my husband's work car.

But that's what we had, so we drove to New Jersey from Richmond in a 2001 Mercury Sable. Oh, did I mention the air conditioner didn't work?

In the middle of the summer heat, we set out on our impromptu getaway. That was the best road trip even without working air conditioner. We rolled the windows down, played our music, and just talked and joked the whole way.

Also, because I stayed with my cousin in New Jersey, I hadn't seen him in a few years, it was good to catch up with him. While I was there, another cousin stopped by for a visit, and we all took a picture together. Little did I know that would be the last picture we would take together.

All in all, 2017 wasn't too bad. Just when you think you can breathe just a little… you guessed it, cancer showed its ugly face for the third time in 2018.

"

Love has no age, no limit; and no death. – John Galsworthy

"

Chapter 6: Everlasting Love

In the spring of 2018, we found out that my husband's lymphoma had returned. One morning after getting off from work, J.O. was sitting on the side of the bed, and it seemed like he was having a hard time breathing. I asked if he was okay, and that's when he told me those dreadful words, "I think the cancer is back."

A little caught off guard and hoping it wasn't true, I asked, "Why do you say that?"

He said, "My urine has been dark like beer."

"When did that start?" I asked. And he said several weeks ago. I immediately said, "Why didn't you tell me?"

I couldn't believe that he kept something like that from me all of that time. But I get it now, he didn't want me to worry; and I must admit, I was very worried! We had gone through two rounds of cancer at that point.

He had some coughing before this, but he went to the doctor, and was told that it was bronchitis. That explained why the coughing wasn't really getting better. It wasn't bronchitis; it was because the lymphoma had returned.

When my husband told me his urine was dark, I immediately felt a sense of fear and mad because he didn't tell me earlier. I got myself together assured my husband, "It's going to be okay. If it has returned, we'll get through it together." I don't know if I really believed it would be okay, but I believed with everything in me that we would get through it together. As always…

J.O. was feeling emotional and upset. He said, "I'm tired, Gina."

I said, "I know, but we aren't going to panic. Let's get an appointment with your hematologist and go from there."

He called his hematologist and scheduled the appointment.

…

Before that appointment though, we were home and I was cooking while watching TV. I heard J.O. sneeze, and then I thought… *that's a long sneeze*.

I peeped around the corner and said, "J.O." He was making this ticking sound, and his head was moving back and forth.

I ran over to him and shook him and said, "J.O… J.O… you okay?"

He looked up and said, "I think so."

I said, "You were shaking and making this ticking sound."

He said, "I was watching TV and could hear the TV, but that's all." He couldn't remember blacking out.

I asked, "That's all you remember?"

He said, "Yes."

Then I said, "I think I should take you to the hospital if you can't remember what happened." So we headed to the hospital.

...

When we arrived at the hospital and J.O. was examined, they admitted him immediately. He was in the hospital for about 10 days; it was found that he had Sepsis—a life threatening disease caused by an infection in the body.[1]

The Sepsis was caused by the lymphoma affecting his liver and spleen again. Of course, they were not certain his lymphoma was back, but all the symptoms were pointing in that direction.

---

[1] Found at https://www.mayoclinic.org/diseases-conditions/sepsis/symptoms-causes/syc-20351214

The process started all over again with many doctor visits, and a bone marrow test to confirm the lymphoma. Each time the lymphoma came back, it was a little bit more aggressive than the time before.

My husband had to suffer through all day fevers, and sweating at night because the fever would break only for a few hours only to rise again. I hated that he had to go through that again.

I wanted cancer to leave him alone.

Finally, after the lymphoma was verified, my husband began chemo to keep him alive until we moved to the decision of having CAR T therapy.

CAR T therapy, or Chimeric antigen receptor T-cell therapy, is a type of treatment in which a patient's T cells are changed in the laboratory so they can attack cancer cells.[2]

The T cells, which created in the lab, are taken from a patient's blood. The gene for a special receptor

[2] Found at https://www.cancer.org/treatment/treatments-and-side-effects/treatment-types/immunotherapy/car-t-cell1.html

that binds to a certain protein on the patient's cancer cells is added to the T cells in the laboratory. The special receptor is called a *Chimeric antigen receptor*.

Many CAR T cells are grown in the laboratory and given to the patient by infusion. I know what you're probably thinking, "Wow."

I know, right. Let's just say my husband was officially a genetically modified human.

We had only two choices to make in order for my husband to have a chance at surviving. The first choice was a bone marrow transplant from a donor or CAR T treatment. We opted for the CAR T treatment.

…

So after months of having fevers, chemo treatments, Mucositis, weight loss, enlarged spleen, it was finally time to be admitted to the hospital and prepare for CAR T.

There is a lot of preparation on CAR T day. The first step was to have conditioning chemo to prepare for the CAR T. This went on for several days.

On the day of the CAR T Treatment, my husband's room was filled with a team of doctors, nurses, hospital news crew; everyone was excited and praying this was the miracle that would cure my husband's lymphoma.

…

J.O. did great through the process. He was monitored very closely for any side effects from the treatment. He did experience high fevers and chills after treatment.

On the days he had a high fever, he had a cooling blanket placed on him. Let me tell you, it was cold! It's literally a plastic blanket filled with water and set on low temperatures to help cool the body.

I felt so bad when he had that blanket on him because he would literally shake. After all, it was so cold. But that cold blanket got the job done, though it's not a pleasant experience to go through.

I was so thankful that CAR T treatment went well because I had to move our eldest son into his dorm for his freshman year of college. I couldn't help but to worry what would happen if my husband started having major side effects and had to be rushed into intensive care while I was in Williamsburg, Virginia with our son.

I had been emotional that week, and the hospital team at MCV Massey Cancer Center assured me they would take care of him. "Don't worry," they said.

Even though they tried to reassure me, I felt like I would feel horrible if I couldn't be there every day. I'd been there since day one. Those were the moments when the doctor tried to calm my fears and helplessness.

In this journey, I learned that God never left us helpless, and He is not the author of fear.

…

J.O. never had to go to intensive care, thank God. So, after about 3 weeks in the hospital, he was released. Just like with the bone marrow transplant, we still had to go to the clinic every day.

His labs were looking great week after week; and finally, tests were done. He was in remission.

The CAR T cells treatment was successful. Before CAR T, my husband's torso was filled with cancer cells; and remarkably, the treatment had killed the lymphoma.

My husband was interviewed on the local news station because he was the very first person to receive CAR T at MCV Massey Cancer Center Center.

I was so proud of him for talking about his journey for everyone to hear. I felt he deserved to have a little celebrity status being that he had gone through so much.

I admired my husband because he was so strong. He never complained about all of the doctor visits, being on many different medications, and being poked with needles; he still smiled when he could.

Shortly after the good news of being in remission, the lymphoma began to fight back and made its way into my husband's organs again.

...

J.O. started to lose weight, he developed jaundice again. He was given a treatment drug for when Car-T failed, but it didn't help. The lymphoma was just too aggressive.

Even though things seemed to be quickly going downhill, I still kept the faith. I wasn't going to let the devil control my thoughts.

A few days before my husband passed, the doctor explained the results of J.O.'s latest scans to us. The results weren't good; yet still I told the doctor that I understood, but I'm still leaving it up to God. We will just see and leave it in God's hands.

◆

Two days later, the doctor met with my mother-in-law and me, and said he wasn't improving but quickly declining.

I felt like someone had punched me in my stomach and was ripping my heart out. All I could do was think of what I was going to do without him. The man I've spent the last 26 years loving, my best friend, was fading away.

I'll never forget that day of talking with the doctor. After talking with the doctor, I went back to my husband's room and sat with him for a while; watching him just sleeping in and out, looking tired.

Before I left his room, I leaned over with tears in my eyes, saying, "I'm going to go, and I'll be back around lunchtime tomorrow."

He said, "In the morning."

I thought that he was confused with the medication, so I lifted his oxygen piece and said, "Did you say in the morning?"

He said, "Yeah, come in the morning."

I could see it was a struggle for him to speak because he was weak. So I joked and said, "Oh, you wanna see your beautiful wife in the morning, huh?"

He said, "Yeah, come morning."

I responded with, "Okay, I will see you in the morning then." I kissed his forehead and said, "I love you."

He responded, "love you, too."

…

I left that room feeling like bricks were weighing me down. I called my best friend and told her what was going on, and she met me at my salon. I couldn't go straight home.

How was I going to look at my son that was home and say, "Daddy isn't going to get better?" Our other son who was at college... I knew I would have to tell him the same. I just didn't know how to face them at that moment.

...

You don't know pain until you have to tell your kids that their dad isn't going to get better, and we have to prepare to say goodbye. I would bear all pain but to have my children in pain is like a knife to the heart.

I couldn't believe that soon he would be gone. Why couldn't cancer leave him alone? And yes, I said with all the evil people in the world, why they get to enjoy life and my husband can't?

I prayed to God that night to take J.O. peacefully, and if this is His will, I don't want my husband to suffer anymore. I love him too much to see him suffer any more. I didn't get any sleep that night.

...

The next morning I got dressed to go to the hospital. As I was getting ready to leave, the hospital called. The nurse told me that the doctor didn't think it would be much longer now…

"Jonathan didn't have a good night."

I told her that I was on my way. I left, heading to the hospital. I called my sister and told her what was going on, and she said, "I'll be down there."

I arrived at the hospital and went into my husband's room. I said, "Hey babe," and he grunted, so I knew he knew I was there.

I kissed his forehead and said, "I love you," and he grunted. I sat there in pure disbelief.

Was this really happening? What was I going to do without my Sweet Daddy? He's been my rock, my piece, and everything for over 25 years.

It just didn't seem real. I just kept praying, "Lord, take him peacefully with You."

Shortly after being at the hospital, family members from both his side and my side of our family showed up, along with one of my friends.

J.O. recognized her voice when she said, "Hey Jay." He grunted.

As family arrived, it was time to tell my kids what was going on. How do you find the words to tell them that their dad will leave because his health has declined, and there is nothing more that can be done?

I still remember talking to them, saying, "We gotta let daddy go because he's been through enough, and we don't want him to suffer anymore."

I will never forget that feeling. I felt like someone pierced my heart with a knife.

So with family and friends around, my husband peacefully passed away on February 15, 2019. That was the day a part of me died with him.

...

I'm not the same woman I was. This woman struggles every day with grief. People have said they really can't imagine what I'm feeling; and my response is, "You're right. If you've never had your soul actually ache with pain, then you can't possibly understand how I feel."

Many people have told me how strong I am. I can't say that I am; all I know is I have two young men to take care of, and they need me to fight to push forward.

◆

My life is totally different... my soul mate, my best friend, my #1 supporter is gone. This is a journey I must handle my way.

Everyone doesn't grieve the same.

Maybe having a necklace or keeping your husband's picture isn't for some, but it is for me. I've chosen to grieve my way and on my terms.

I am a strong supporter of having a therapist to help through the grieving process.

All in all, my love for J.O. will last eternally. I'm grateful for the time we've shared; and I only pray that my sons will walk boldly and proudly in their father's shoes — they are mighty big shoes to fill!

To Be Continued...

"

My mission in life is not merely to survive, but to thrive; and to do so with some passion, some compassion, some humor, and some style. – Maya Angelou

"

About the Authors

Regina "Queen" Newby is novelist and award-winning hairstylist out of Richmond, Virginia. Born in Goochland, Virginia, she graduated from Goochland High and attended Virginia School of Cosmetology immediately after. She has worked for over 27 years in the beauty industry.

Outside of her hair career, Regina is a cancer and special needs advocate, as well as dedicated mother to sons Jonathan (Alex) and Braxton, and lifelong follower of Christ.

She owns a beauty product line, Nine7, dedicated to her soulmate and late husband Jonathan (J.O.) who passed away from a long battle with large b cell lymphoma.

…

Jonathan "J.O." Newby was raised in Surry County, and graduated Surry High School in 1991, going on to earn a bachelor's degree in Hotel and Restaurant from Norfolk State University.

Before his passing, he was a longtime employee of United Parcel Service, and started his own family business, Sweet Daddyz Cookies.

Queen and J.O. were married on September 7, 1996. They enjoyed spending time together watching movies and going on spur-of-the-moment dates.

After J.O. passed, Regina became sure of this one thing: his story will be told.

Acknowledgements

I would like to thank all of our family and friends who prayed and supported us. Every prayer and donation that was ever given meant so much to the both of us.

I thank the team of doctors and staff who cared for my husband at MCV Massey Cancer Center. The care he received was impeccable and I will forever be grateful.

I want to also thank Dr. Ghulam Quereshi for not giving up and first diagnosing my husband. We were given more years with my husband because of the care of his doctors, nurses and support staff. A thousand thank you's would never be enough.

I ask that everyone that reads this book will continue to pray for my family as we navigate through life without him.